THE COOK'S COLLECTION
❀
DELIGHTFUL
DESSERTS

Author: Annette Wolter

Photography: Susi and Pete Eising, Odette Teubner,
  Rolf Feuz and Karin Messerli

Translated by UPS Translations, London

Edited by Josephine Bacon

CLB 4156

This edition published in 1995 by Grange Books

an imprint of Grange Books PLC, The Grange, Grange Yard, London SE1 3AG

This material published originally under the series title "Kochen Wie Noch Nie"
by Gräfe und Unzer Verlag GmbH, München

© 1995 Gräfe und Unzer Verlag GmbH, München

English translation copyright: © 1995 by CLB Publishing, Godalming, Surrey

Typeset by Image Setting, Brighton, E. Sussex

Printed and bound in Singapore

ISBN 1-85627-775-5

THE COOK'S COLLECTION

❈

DELIGHTFUL DESSERTS

Annette Wolter

Grange
BOOKS

Introduction

Whether you wish to provide a spectacular finale to an elaborate dinner party or simply want to round off a family meal, you are sure to find a dessert to suit your requirements among this wonderful collection of recipes. These desserts range from substantial cakes, pies and creamy puddings to flans and refreshing fruit dishes.

With so many different and exotic varieties of fruit now available in supermarkets, such as lychees, star fruit and kumquats, the scope for vitamin-rich fruit desserts has widened dramatically in recent years. Fruit recipes have the added advantage of versatility, as you can often use whatever fruit you have to hand rather than the one specified.

In this book, low-fat alternatives to cream are frequently used. Many people who are advised to cut down on their fat intake will be surprised to discover that the desserts in this book made with yogurt or quark taste just as good as those made with cream.

Whatever type of dessert you need, this book is a wonderful source of fresh ideas that you are sure to enjoy experimenting with. In the opinion of many, a meal without a dessert is not a proper meal, and a special occasion is not special without a selection of the finest dessert dishes.

Rich Raspberry Cream

500g/1lb 2oz raspberries
4 tbsps icing sugar
3 tbsps grappa or raspberry
liqueur
2 eggs
250g/8oz mascarpone or full-
fat cream cheese
100ml/3 fl oz single cream
2 sponge fingers

Preparation time:
30 minutes
Chilling time:
2 hours
Nutritional value:
Analysis per serving, approx:
• 1800kJ/430kcal
• 11g protein
• 29g fat
• 26g carbohydrate

Rinse the raspberries several times in a bowl of water. • Drain and carefully mix with 2 tbsps of sifted icing sugar and the grappa. • Separate the eggs. Beat the yolks with the remaining icing sugar until fluffy. • Gradually add the mascarpone to the egg yolks and continue beating until a thick cream is formed. • Whisk the egg whites until stiff; whip the cream until stiff and fold both into the mascarpone cream. • Alternate layers of the cream with the raspberries in four dessert glasses, finishing with a layer of the cream mixture. Refrigerate. • Wrap the sponge fingers in cling film and crush with a rolling pin. Sprinkle the crumbs over the dessert before serving.

Orange Cream

*4 leaves gelatine or 2 tsps
powdered gelatine
350ml/4 fl oz water
500g/1lb 2oz juicy oranges
4 egg yolks
50g/2oz sugar
1 tbsp vanilla sugar
2 tbsps Cointreau
2 egg whites
125ml/4 fl oz whipping cream*

Preparation time:
30 minutes
Nutritional value:
Analysis per serving, approx:
• 1300kJ/310kcal
• 18g protein
• 22g fat
• 32g carbohydrate

Soak the leaf gelatine in the cold water. • Wash one orange in warm water, dry it and grate the rind. Reserve in the refrigerator. Squeeze the juice from all the oranges. • Beat the egg yolks with the sugar and vanilla sugar until fluffy. • Heat the orange juice. Press the liquid from the leaf gelatine and dissolve the gelatine in the hot orange juice (if using powdered gelatine, follow directions on packet). Combine this with the Cointreau and stir into the egg yolk mixture with the orange rind. • Place in the refrigerator. • Whisk the egg whites until stiff. Whip the cream until stiff. • Place two tbsps whipped cream in a piping-bag and fold the rest of the cream and the egg whites into the orange cream. Arrange in individual dessert bowls or glasses. • Peel half an orange very thinly and cut the rind into very fine julienne strips. Decorate the pudding with rosettes of cream and the reserved grated orange rind. Sprinkle with julienned orange.

Mocha Cream

2 eggs
1 tsp cocoa powder
500ml/16 fl oz milk
6 leaves gelatine or 1 tsp
powdered gelatine
250ml/8 fl oz water
4 tbsps sugar
1 tbsp vanilla sugar
5 tsps instant coffee powder
250ml/8 fl oz whipping cream
50g/2oz chocolate-flavoured
coffee beans

Preparation time:
40 minutes
Chilling time:
1 hour
Nutritional value:
Analysis per serving, approx:
• 2010kJ/480kcal
• 16g protein
• 34g fat
• 28g carbohydrate

Separate the eggs. • Blend the egg yolks with the cocoa powder and four tbsps milk until smooth. • Soak the gelatine in the cold water. • Bring 250ml/8 fl oz milk to the boil with the sugar, vanilla sugar and coffee powder, stirring constantly. When it boils, remove from the heat. • Whisk the egg yolk mixture into the mocha milk. Press the liquid from the gelatine and dissolve the gelatine in the mocha milk, or combine 125ml/4 fl oz of the mocha milk with the powdered gelatine then mix well with the rest of the mocha milk • Refrigerate the mixture. • Whip the cream until stiff and chill it. • Whisk the egg whites until stiff and fold into the mocha milk once it begins to thicken. • Take two-thirds of the whipped cream, add to the setting mixture and stir it in with a spoon in swirls so that a marbled pattern results. • Place the mixture in dessert glasses and leave to set firmly in the refrigerator. • Decorate with the remaining whipped cream and chocolate-flavoured coffee beans.

Filled Orange Halves

4 oranges
50g/2oz shelled walnuts
1 banana
100g/4oz chocolate sweetened
with cane sugar
250ml/8 fl oz whipping cream
1 tbsp cocoa powder
1 tbsp orange blossom honey

Preparation time:
50 minutes
Nutritional value:
Analysis per serving, approx:
• 2200kJ/520kcal
• 7g protein
• 36g fat
• 46g carbohydrate

Wash the oranges in warm water, dry them and cut in half crossways. Use a sharp-edged teaspoon to scoop out the flesh; place it in a sieve to drain. • Remove the pips from the fruit. • Remove the skin from the orange halves and cut a thin sliver of peel from the round end of each orange half so that they will sit flat. • Place two halves on each dessert plate. • Chop the walnuts coarsely and roast in a dry pan, turning them until they darken and smell good. • Peel the banana, cut in half lengthways and slice. • Break the chocolate into pieces, melt with 100ml/3 fl oz cream in a bowl over a pan of simmering water on a low heat and stir in the cocoa powder. • Leave half the mixture over the pan of hot water. • Mix the rest of the chocolate with the banana slices, nuts, honey and orange pulp. • Whip the rest of the cream until stiff, fold into the orange mixture, divide among the orange halves and sprinkle with the remaining chocolate.

Quince Foam

2 leaves gelatine or 1 tsp
powdered gelatine
125ml/4 fl oz water (omit if
using powdered gelatine)
300g/10oz quinces
300g/10oz cooking apples
½ vanilla pod
1 cinnamon stick
¼ tsp coriander seeds
300ml/14 fl oz water
70g/3oz orange blossom honey
200ml/6 fl oz whipping cream
2 tbsps orange liqueur
40g/1½oz shelled walnuts

Preparation time:
50 minutes
Chilling time:
1 hour
Nutritional value:
Analysis per serving, approx:
• 1600kJ/380kcal
• 4g protein
• 23g fat
• 38g carbohydrate

Soak the leaf gelatine in the cold water. • Wash the quinces and apples thoroughly in lukewarm water and chop coarsely, leaving the peel on. • Split the vanilla pod and scrape out the inside. Place both with the fruit, the cinnamon stick, the coriander and the water in a covered saucepan over a medium heat and cook for at least 20 minutes. • Remove the vanilla pod and cinnamon. • Pass the fruit through a fine sieve. • Squeeze the gelatine and add it to the fruit purée or add the teaspoon of powdered gelatine to the purée. Mix the honey into the purée and leave to cool. • Whip the cream until stiff and mix with the orange liqueur. • Chop the walnuts. • Stir two-thirds of the whipped cream into the fruit purée and place in four dessert glasses or a serving bowl and refrigerate. • Decorate with the remaining whipped cream and sprinkle with the chopped nuts before serving.

Caramel Apples with Calvados

4 cooking apples
2 tsps lemon juice
150g/5¹/₂oz sugar
1 clove
175ml/5 fl oz still mineral water
200ml/7 fl oz Calvados

Preparation time:
40 minutes
Marinating time:
1 hour
Nutritional value:
Analysis per serving, approx:
• 980kJ/230kcal•
• 1g protein
• 1g fat
• 54g carbohydrate

Peel and quarter the apples. Remove the cores, slice the quarters and sprinkle with lemon juice. • Reserve 3 tbsps of the mineral water in a separate pan. Heat up 100g/4oz of the sugar with the clove and the rest of the mineral water in a saucepan, stirring until the sugar is completely dissolved. • Add the slices of apple to the syrup, cover and simmer over a gentle heat for 15 minutes. Transfer the apple mixture to a shallow bowl. • Remove the clove and boil the syrup, uncovered, until it thickens. Remove from the heat, add the Calvados and pour this over the apple segments. • Allow the apples to cool, then cover and leave in the refrigerator to marinate. • Melt the remaining sugar with the reserved mineral water in a pan over a low heat; bring to the boil stirring constantly and continue stirring until the sugar has caramelised to a light brown. • Drizzle the caramel in thin threads over the apple.

Cold Melon Soup

2 leaves gelatine or 1 tsp
powdered gelatine
125ml/4 fl oz water (omit if
using powdered gelatine)
1 charentais and 1 honeydew
melon each weighing 750g/1lb
10oz
2 oranges
100g/4oz raw cane sugar
1 lemon
2 tbsps orange liqueur
1 sprig of lemon balm
(optional)
Ice cubes

Preparation time:
20 minutes
Chilling time:
1 hour
Nutritional value:
Analysis per serving, approx:
• 990kJ/240kcal
• 5g protein
• 0g fat
• 52g carbohydrate

quarter of each melon using a
melon baller. • Peel the
remaining quarters and cut the
flesh into small cubes. •
Squeeze the juice from the
oranges, add with the sugar to
the melon quarters, and purée
the mixture. • Wash the lemon
in warm water, dry and peel
thinly. Cut the rind into very
fine julienne strips. • Squeeze
the lemon juice and heat it. •
Squeeze out the gelatine and
add it to the lemon juice or
dissolve the powdered gelatine
in the hot lemon juice. Add
with the orange liqueur to the
fruit purée. • Add the melon
balls to the cold soup and chill
before serving. • Rinse the
lemon balm in lukewarm
water, wipe it dry, pull off
leaves and sprinkle them over
the soup with the crushed ice
cubes.

Soak the leaf gelatine in the
cold water. • Quarter the
melons and remove the seeds.
Scoop out the flesh from one

Charlotte Royal

Ingredients for 12 portions:
For the Swiss roll mixture:
6 egg yolks
100g/4oz sugar
1 tbsp vanilla sugar
4 egg whites
Pinch of salt
100g/4oz flour
25g/1oz cornflour
For spreading:
480g/1lb 2oz raspberry jam
2 tbsps raspberry liqueur
For the cream:
7 leaves gelatine or 1 packet powdered gelatine
500ml/16 fl oz water
4 egg yolks
100g/4oz sugar
½ vanilla pod
Juice of 1 orange and 1 lemon
250ml/8 fl oz dry white wine
2 egg whites
Pinch of salt
250ml/8 fl oz cream
Extra sugar for sprinkling

Preparation time:
1¼ hours
Chilling time:
5 hours
Nutritional value:
Analysis per serving, approx:
• 1590kJ/380kcal
• 9g protein
• 12g fat
• 55g carbohydrate

Heat the oven to 220°C/425°F/Gas Mark 7. Use an electric beater to beat the egg yolks with 50g/2oz sugar and the vanilla sugar until the sugar has dissolved completely. Sift the flour and cornflour over the mixture and fold them in. • Whisk the egg whites with the salt until fluffy, then add the rest of the sugar and continue beating until stiff and glossy. Line a Swiss roll tin with baking parchment. • Fold the egg whites into the egg yolk mixture. • Spread the Swiss roll mixture on the baking sheet and bake for about 12 minutes on the upper shelf of

the oven until golden. •
Sprinkle a kitchen towel with
sugar, turn the Swiss roll onto
the cloth, pull off the paper
and cover the sponge with a
damp cloth. • Stir the jam and
the raspberry liqueur over a
low heat until smooth, pass
through a sieve and spread
over the sponge. • Use the
cloth to roll up the Swiss roll
and leave to cool under the
damp cloth. Now make the
cream. • Soak leaf gelatine in
the cold water. • Whisk the
egg yolks with the sugar until
fluffy. Split the vanilla pod
lengthways, scrape out the
inside and stir into the egg
yolk mixture. • Strain the fruit
juice and heat it. • Press the
liquid from the leaf gelatine
and dissolve in the warm juice
(if using powdered gelatine,
follow directions on packet). •
Stir the wine into the egg yolk
mixture and gradually whisk in
the gelatine mixture. Place the
mixture in the refrigerator. •
Whisk the egg whites with the
salt until stiff. Whip the cream

until stiff. • As soon as the egg
yolk mixture begins to
thicken, whisk the egg whites
and whipped cream into the
mixture and return to the
refrigerator. • Cut the Swiss
roll into 1cm/½-inch-thick
slices and use them to line a
bowl. Fill the mould with the
cream mixture. • Leave to chill
for at least five hours. • To
serve, unmould onto a serving
dish and cut into 12 equal
slices like a gateau.

Our Tip: *You can use the leftover*
egg whites to make meringues:
whisk the egg whites with
200g/7oz caster or icing sugar and
3 tsps cornflour until stiff and pipe
or spoon onto a baking tray lined
with baking parchment. Dry rather
than bake for two hours at
100°C/200°F/Gas Mark 1/4
in the oven, leaving the oven door
ajar. Remove the meringues from
the oven, leave to cool completely
and store in an airtight tin.

Chocolate Ice Cream Roll

Ingredients for 1 roll:
For the ice cream:
6 egg yolks
75g/3oz sugar
150g/5¹/₂oz plain chocolate
250ml/8 fl oz whipping cream
For the roll:
8 egg yolks
100g/4oz sugar
4 egg whites
80g/3oz flour
20g/3/4oz cornflour
100ml/3 fl oz whipping cream
1 tbsp vanilla sugar
2 tbsps chocolate strands

Preparation time:
45 minutes
Freezing time:
3 hours
Baking:
12 minutes
Nutritional value:
Analysis per serving (serves 12):
• 2390kJ/570kcal
• 20g protein
• 41g fat
• 28g carbohydrate

Beat the egg yolks and sugar until fluffy. • Break the chocolate into pieces and melt with half the cream. Cool and beat into the egg yolk mixture until it thickens. • Whip the rest of the cream until stiff and fold into the chocolate mixture. • Cover with aluminium foil and freeze for two hours. • Meanwhile, make the sponge. Heat the oven to 220°C/425°F/Gas Mark 7. Line the baking sheet with baking parchment. • Beat the egg yolks and sugar until fluffy. Whisk the egg whites until stiff and fold into the egg yolk mixture with the flour and cornflour. • Spread the mixture onto the baking sheet and bake for 12 minutes until golden. • Turn out the sponge onto a tea towel sprinkled with sugar, pull off the paper and cover the sponge with a damp cloth; leave to cool. • Allow the ice cream to soften slightly and spread it over the sponge. • Roll up the sponge and return it to the freezer. • Whip the

cream and vanilla sugar until
stiff, spread it on the sponge
roll and decorate with
chocolate strands.

17

Raspberry Charlotte

Ingredients for one 18cm/7-inch soufflé dish:

For the charlotte:
350g/11oz crème fraîche
400g/14oz raspberries
5 leaves of gelatine or 2½ tsps powdered
250ml/8 fl oz water (omit if using powdered)
1 vanilla pod
250ml/8 fl oz milk
Pinch of salt
4 tbsps sugar
4 egg yolks
1 tsp butter
1 tsp sugar
21 sponge fingers

For the sauce:
400g/14oz raspberries
2 tbsps icing sugar
1 tbsp lemon juice
200ml/6 fl oz raspberry liqueur

Preparation time:
1 hour
Chilling time:
12 hours
Nutritional value:
Analysis per serving (serves 8):
• 2180kJ/520kcal
• 13g protein
• 34g fat
• 39g carbohydrate

Chill the crème fraîche in the refrigerator before use.
• Wash the raspberries in a bowl of water and skim the dirt from the surface, then drain them in a sieve. • Soak the leaf gelatine in the cold water. • Split the vanilla pod lengthwise and scrape out the inside with a knife. • Bring the milk, the vanilla and pod halves, salt and sugar to the boil, stirring all the time. Remove from the heat and stir in the egg yolks one at a time.

Return the milk to the heat and continue stirring until the mixture thickens, but do not allow it to boil. • Squeeze the liquid from the gelatine, blend into the hot mixture and allow it to cool, stirring frequently (if using powdered, follow directions on packet). • Refrigerate the mixture until it sets. • Brush the base and sides of the dish with butter and sprinkle with the sugar. Arrange the sponge fingers vertically around the round edge facing outwards. Reserve one sponge finger. • Whisk the crème fraîche. Also whisk the egg mixture and stir into the crème fraîche, little by little, until it is well blended. • Place one-third of the mixture in the dish which has been lined with sponge fingers. Next add a layer of the raspberries followed by another layer of

the cream mixture, the remaining raspberries and finishing with the remaining mixture. • Crumble the one remaining sponge finger and sprinkle over the top. • Cover the mould and leave in the refrigerator, preferably overnight, but for at least six hours. • To make the sauce: wash and drain the 400g/14oz raspberries. Keep about 20 raspberries for decoration. • Strain the other raspberries through a fine sieve and mix with the icing sugar, lemon juice and raspberry liqueur, or purée it all in a food processor or liquidiser. • Shortly before serving, dip the bowl briefly in hot water, turn out the charlotte onto a serving plate and decorate the top with the remaining raspberries. Serve the fruit sauce as an accompaniment.

Tropical Cream Cheese Gâteau

Quantities for 1 28cm/11in tin
3 eggs
50g/2oz sugar
1 tbsp vanilla sugar
50g/2oz flour
25g/1oz cornflour
25g/1oz ground hazelnuts
1 packet unflavoured gelatine
500g/1lb 2oz low-fat quark
250g/8oz full-fat cream cheese or mascarpone
100g/4oz sugar
125ml/4fl oz thick-set yogurt
3 tbsps advocaat
Rind and juice of 1 lemon
400ml/15 fl oz whipping cream
2 tbsps amaretto liqueur
1 large mango
4 kiwis
125g/4oz flaked almonds
for the topping:
250ml/8 fl oz whipping cream
4 tbsps icing sugar
2 kiwis
1 medium mango

Preparation time:
6 hours
Baking time:
20 minutes
Nutritional value:
Analysis per slice, approx, if divided into 16 slices:
• 1300kJ/310kcal
• 12g protein
• 17g fat
• 24g carbohydrate

Heat the oven to 180°C/350°F/Gas Mark 4. • Separate the eggs and whisk the whites until stiff. Beat the yolks with the sugar and vanilla sugar. Fold the flour, cornflour, hazelnuts and whisked whites into the beaten yolks. Bake for 20 minutes. • Dissolve the gelatine in 125ml/4 fl oz hot water. • Drain the quark and then mix with the cream cheese, sugar, yogurt, advocaat and grated lemon rind. • Heat lemon juice with 2 tbsps water. Add the gelatine to the hot lemon water and quark mixture and leave in the refrigerator until partially set. • Whip the cream and stir it into the cheese mixture. • Sprinkle the sponge with amaretto and return to the tin. Line the base and rim

of the tin. • Arrange kiwi and mango slices alternately on the sponge base. Spread the cheese mixture over them. Toast the almonds and press them around the cake. Refrigerate for 4 hours until set. Whip cream with icing sugar until stiff, and pipe over cake. Decorate with the kiwi and mango.

21

Raspberry Cream Gâteau

Quantities for 1 26cm/10in springform tin

For the sponge:
6 eggs
Pinch of salt
150g/5¹/₂oz sugar
175g/6oz flour
75g/3oz cornflour
2 tsps baking powder

For the filling and decorations:
50g/2oz flaked almonds
¹/₂ packet unflavoured gelatine
250g/8oz low-fat quark
Zest of ¹/₂ lemon
3 tbsps maple syrup
2 tbsps vanilla sugar
500ml/18 fl oz whipping cream
1 tbsp lemon juice
600g/1lb 6oz raspberries
3 tbsps icing sugar
4 tbsps raspberry jam
2 tbsps raspberry liqueur
25g/1oz chopped pistachio nuts

Preparation time:
30 minutes
Baking time:
30 minutes

Resting time:
at least 6 hours
Final preparations:
45 mins
Nutritional value:
Analysis per slice, approx, if divided into 16 slices:
• 1260kJ/300kcal
• 7g protein
• 14g fat
• 22g carbohydrate

Heat the oven to 180°C/350°F/Gas Mark 4. Butter the base of the springform tin and sprinkle with breadcrumbs. • Separate the eggs. Whisk the whites with the salt until they are stiff but not dry. Beat the egg yolks and sugar until the sugar has completely dissolved. Pour the whisked eggs on top of the beaten eggs and fold them in. Mix the flour, cornflour and baking powder and sift the mixture over the beaten egg mixture; fold them in. • Pour the sponge mixture into the tin, smooth the surface and bake on the middle shelf for 30 minutes, or until golden. •

Switch off the oven and leave to rest for 5 minutes. Remove from the oven and leave for a further 10 minutes. Unmould the tin onto a cake rack and leave for at least 6 hours. • Toast the flaked almonds in a dry frying pan until golden brown and leave to cool. • Dissolve the gelatine in 125ml/4 fl oz hot water. Combine the quark, grated lemon rind, maple syrup and vanilla sugar. Whip the cream until stiff. Fold 100g/4oz whipped cream into the quark. • Warm the lemon juice with 2 tbsps water. Remove from the heat and add the dissolved gelatine. Gradually add the quark to half of the liquid gelatine. Slowly add the other half of the gelatine liquid to the remaining whipped cream. • Wash the raspberries, dry well and purée 250g/8oz of them with the icing sugar. • Fit a star nozzle to a piping bag and fill with one third of the whipped cream. Mix the rest of the cream with the puréed raspberries. • Cut the sponge cake in half crossways to make two layers. Stir the raspberry liqueur into the raspberry jam. Brush this over the bottom layer of the cake. Spread the rest of the quark mixture on top, cover with the top half of the cake and press lightly. • Coat the surface and sides of the cake with raspberry cream. Press the flaked almonds into the sides. • Arrange the remaining raspberries on top, dot the edge of the cake with cream whirls and sprinkle each with pistachio nuts. • Refrigerate until ready to serve.

Our tip: To make the torte higher and even more impressive, bake a thin base of shortcrust pastry in the same tin. Brush it with raspberry jam and place the sponge mixture on top.

23

Iced Cheesecake

Ingredients for a 26cm/10-inch springform cake tin:
200g/7oz sponge fingers
50g/2oz butter
1 tbsp vanilla sugar
Generous pinch of ground cinnamon
3 egg yolks
100g/4oz icing sugar
2 tbsps lemon juice
Grated rind of $1/2$ a lemon
500g/1lb 2oz mascarpone (Italian cream cheese)
250ml/8 fl oz whipping cream
2 tbsps cocoa powder
12 cocktail cherries

Preparation time:
45 minutes
Freezing time:
3 hours
Nutritional value:
Analysis per serving (serves 12):
• 1890kJ/450kcal
• 12g protein
• 33g fat
• 24g carbohydrate

Crush the sponge fingers with a rolling pin between sheets of cling film • Melt the butter and mix into the sponge crumbs with the vanilla sugar and cinnamon. Line the base of the tin, pressing the dough down firmly. • Beat the egg yolks with the icing sugar until fluffy and mix in the lemon juice, rind and the mascarpone. Stir 125ml/4 fl oz cream into the mixture. • Spread the mixture over the sponge base, cover with aluminium foil and freeze for about three hours to set. • Whip the remaining cream until stiff and place in a piping bag with a star nozzle. • Loosen the edge of the cheesecake from the tin with a sharp knife. Sift cocoa powder over the top and slide it onto a cake plate. Decorate with rosettes of cream and cocktail cherries.

Our Tip: *Mascarpone can be replaced by any cream cheese, such as Philadelphia, but this will give a firmer consistency. To achieve the same consistency, add 200ml/6 fl oz double cream instead of 125ml/4 fl oz.*

Summer Fruit Flan

Quantities for 1 24cm/9½in
flan
250g/8oz self-raising flour
1 egg
75g/3oz sugar
Pinch of salt
125g/5oz butter, diced
100g/4oz marzipan
75g/3oz icing sugar
250g/8oz strawberries
200g/7oz raspberries
125g/5oz each blackberries
and redcurrants
100g/4oz blackcurrants
2 packets lemon jelly glaze
250ml/8 fl oz each red fruit
juice and water
4 tbsps sugar

Preparation time:
45 minutes
Baking time:
25 minutes
Nutritional value:
Analysis per slice, approx, if
divided into 8 slices:
• 1890kJ/450kcal
• 8g protein
• 18g fat
• 65g carbohydrate

Mix the flour with the egg, sugar, salt and butter to make a smooth dough. Leave to stand for 30 minutes. • Knead the marzipan with 50g/2oz icing sugar. Roll out a circle of marzipan the size of the tin on a surface dusted with the remaining icing sugar, • Wash all the berries and leave to drain; halve any large strawberries and remove the tiny stalks from the redcurrants. Mix the fruits. • Heat the oven to 200°C/400°F/Gas Mark 6. • Roll out a circle of dough and use it to line the tin. Prick all over with a fork. Trim off any excess dough. Sprinkle with dried beans and bake blind for 25 minutes, or until lightly browned. When cool, place on a tray and line with the marzipan. Arrange the fruit on top. • Prepare the jelly glaze with the remaining ingredients, pour this over the fruit and leave to set. in a cool place.

Rhubarb Cake
with an Almond Meringue

Quantities for 1 26cm/10in
springform tin
150g/5¹/₂oz softened butter
300g/11oz sugar
1 tbsp vanilla sugar
5 eggs
150g/5¹/₂oz flour
75g/3oz cornflour
1¹/₂ tsps baking powder
600g/1lb 6oz rhubarb
Pinch of salt
50g/2oz ground almonds
1 tbsp lemon juice

Preparation time:
30 minutes
Baking time:
45 minutes
Nutritional value:
Analysis per slice, approx, if
divided into 12 slices:
• 1380kJ/330kcal
• 7g protein
• 15g fat
• 43g carbohydrate

Cream the butter with 125g/5oz of the sugar and the vanilla sugar. Separate 3 of the eggs. Beat the 2 remaining whole eggs with the egg yolks and gradually add to the creamed butter. Mix the baking powder and cornflour with the flour and add to the egg and butter mixture. • Heat the oven to 180°C/350°F/Gas Mark 4. Butter the tin. • Rinse the rhubarb, trim the ends and strip off the stringy fibres. Cut the sticks into 4cm/1¹/₂in lengths. • Lay the dough in the tin and arrange the rhubarb lengths on top, pressing each piece down a little into the dough. Bake for 25 minutes on the middle shelf. Whisk the egg whites with the salt until they form soft peaks. Add the rest of the sugar and whisk for a little longer until it stands in stiff peaks. • Add the ground almonds and lemon juice. • Pipe or spoon the whisked egg mixture over the cake. • Bake for a further 20 minutes.

Damson Flan

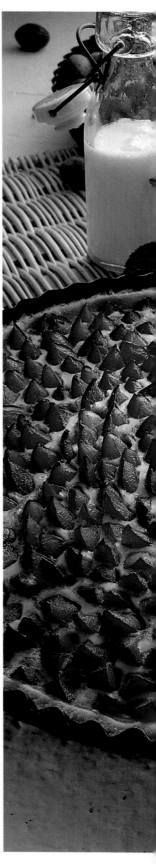

*Quantities for 1 28cm/11in
springform tin
250g/8oz flour
50g/2oz sugar
Generous pinch of salt
100g/4oz butter, diced
8 tbsps cold water
2 tsps vinegar
1kg/2¼lbs damsons
125ml/4 fl oz cream
2 eggs
Generous pinch of ground
cinnamon*

Preparation time:
50 minutes
Baking time:
35 minutes
Nutritional value:
Analysis per slice, approx, if
divided into 12 slices:
• 1090kJ/260kcal
• 5g protein
• 12g fat
• 33g carbohydrate

Mix the flour with 1 tbsp sugar, the salt, butter, water and vinegar. Make a dough using a food mixer or food processor, then use cold hands to make a smooth shortcrust dough. Wrap in clingfilm and leave in the refrigerator for 30 minutes to chill. • Rinse, drain, halve and stone the damsons. • Butter the tin. Heat the oven to 220°/450°F/Gas Mark 7. • Roll out the dough into a circle on a floured work top. Line the tin with the dough, pinching up a 2cm/1in rim. Arrange the damsons close together in a circular pattern on the dough, cut sides upwards. • Bake on the middle shelf of the oven for 10 minutes. • Stir the remaining sugar and cinnamon into the eggs and cream and pour this over the damsons. Bake for a further 25 minutes. If required, sprinkle a few sugar crystals over the cooled surface before serving.

Chiffon Pie

Ingredients for a 24-cm/10-inch flan dish:
100g/4oz nut paste
8 rusks
100g/4oz marzipan
1 tsp ground ginger
5 leaves or 2 tsps powdered gelatine
250ml/8 fl oz water
250ml/8 fl oz orange juice
Grated rind of 1 orange
Juice of 1 lemon
4 eggs
100g/4oz sugar
200ml/6 fl oz whipping cream
4 tbsps orange liqueur
1 tbsp chopped pistachios

Preparation time:
1½ hours
Cooling:
2 hours
Nutritional value:
Analysis per serving (serves 8):
• 1700kJ/400kcal
• 11g protein
• 21g fat
• 42g carbohydrate

Melt the nut paste over a pan of simmering water. • Remove from the heat. Crush the rusks. • Mix the marzipan with the paste, rusks and ginger. • Line the base and edges of a pie dish with this mixture and cool for one hour. • Soak the gelatine leaves in the water. • Boil the orange juice and rind and the lemon juice. • Separate the eggs. Mix 50g/2oz sugar with the egg yolks over a pan of simmering water until creamy. • Squeeze the liquid from the gelatine and dissolve in the fruit juice, (if using powdered, follow directions on packet) and stir into the egg yolk mixture. Leave to cool. • Whisk the egg whites and the rest of the sugar until stiff. • Whip the cream until stiff and stir in the liqueur. • Fold the egg whites and whipped cream into the mixture as it starts to set, place in the pie dish and refrigerate for at least two hours.

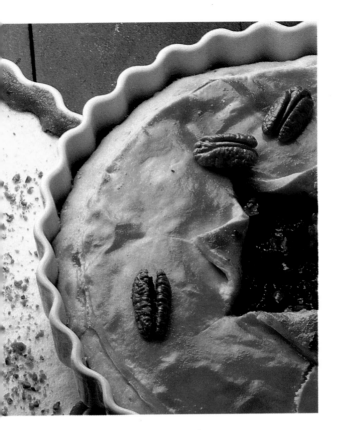

Pecan Pie

Ingredients for a 24cm/10-in pie:
150g/5¹/₂oz cold butter
300g/10oz flour
Pinch of salt
1 egg yolk
For the filling:
4 eggs·
300g/10oz golden syrup
40g/1¹/₂oz flour
60g/2oz butter
1 tsp vanilla essence
400g/14oz pecan nuts, halved

Preparation time:
45 minutes
Baking:
30 minutes
Nutritional value:
Analysis per serving (serves 10):
• 3230kJ/770kcal
• 27g protein
• 58g fat
• 76g carbohydrate

Make a shortcrust pastry with the butter, flour and salt, egg yolk and about 2 tbsps of cold water. • Cover and leave in the refrigerator for 30 minutes to rest. • Heat the oven to180°C/350°F/Gas Mark 4. • Whisk the eggs and stir in the syrup. • Stir the flour, melted butter, vanilla and nuts into the syrup. • Roll out the dough and cut out 2 circles of 24 and 28 cm/10 and 11 ins in diameter respectively. • Line the flan dish with the larger circle of pastry. • Fill with the nut mixture, cover with the smaller circle and press the edges together. • Cut a star shape in the middle of the pie top and fold the points of the star back so that the nut filling is visible. • Bake the pie for 30 minutes.

Clafoutis

75g/3oz flour
3 eggs
200ml/6 fl oz milk
2 tbsps butter
500g/1lb 2oz black cherries,
stoned
Pinch of salt
4 tbsps sugar
Butter for the dish

Preparation time:
1 hour
Cooking time:
45 minutes
Nutritional value:
Analysis per serving, approx:
• 2000kJ/480kcal
• 15g protein
• 22g fat
• 54g carbohydrate

Heat the oven to 190°C/375°F/Gas Mark 5. Sift the flour into a bowl. • Separate one of the eggs. • Add the egg yolk and the other eggs into the flour and gradually add the milk to make a smooth batter. • Melt the butter and gradually stir it into the batter. • Leave the batter covered at room temperature for 30 minutes. • Wash the cherries and and pat dry. • Butter a shallow, ovenproof dish. • Beat the egg white with the salt until stiff and fold into the batter. • Pour the batter into the baking dish, arrange the cherries on top and allow them to sink in. • Bake the clafoutis on the middle shelf of the oven for 20 minutes. Sprinkle the clafoutis with the sugar and bake for a further 20 minutes. • Turn off the oven and leave the soufflé to stand in it for a further five minutes.

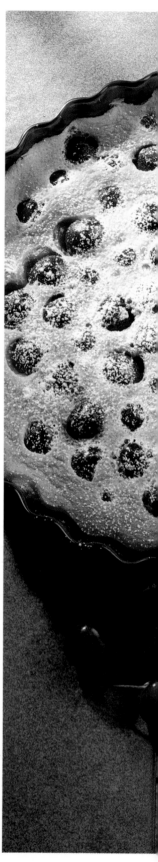

Sweet Cheese Pancakes

For the batter:
125g/5oz flour
Pinch of salt
2 eggs
1 tbsp oil
250ml/8 fl oz milk
1 tsp vanilla sugar
For the filling:
250g/8oz quark
50g/2oz softened butter
50g/2oz sugar
2 egg yolks
½ tsp grated lemon rind
5 tbsps sour cream
75g/3oz raisins, washed
3 egg whites
1 tbsp vanilla sugar
For the glaze:
125ml/4 fl oz milk
1 egg yolk
1 tsp sugar
100g/4oz butter
For topping:
2 tbsps sugar
1 tsp ground cinnamon

Preparation time:
1½ hours
Cooking time:
30 minutes

Nutritional value:
Analysis per serving, approx:
• 3700kJ/880kcal
• 32g protein
• 53g fat
• 66g carbohydrate

Mix all ingredients for the batter, cover and leave to stand for 30 minutes. • Drain the quark in a sieve. • Cream butter and sugar until fluffy. Combine the egg yolks with the lemon rind, quark, sour cream and raisins and add to the creamed butter mix. • Whisk the egg whites with the vanilla sugar until stiff and fold into the quark mixture. • Melt a little butter and cook eight thin pancakes. • Heat the oven to 180°C/350°F/Gas Mark 4. • Spread some of the mixture over each pancake, roll up, cut in half and place in a buttered dish, overlapping one another. • Whisk the milk, egg yolk and sugar and pour over the pancakes. Bake for 30 mins. Sprinkle with the cinna- mon and sugar mixture and serve.

Sweet Pancakes with Nut Cream

For the batter:
150g/5¹/₂oz flour
Pinch of salt
2 eggs
1 egg yolk
250ml/8 fl oz milk
For the filling:
100g/4oz plain chocolate
200ml/6 fl oz whipping cream
1 egg white
1 tbsp vanilla sugar
1 tbsp rum
150g/5¹/₂oz ground hazelnuts
For cooking:
75g/3oz butter

Preparation time:
1 hour
Nutritional value:
Analysis per serving, approx:
• 3600kJ/860kcal
• 24g protein
• 59g fat
• 54g carbohydrate

Make a batter with the flour, salt, eggs, egg yolk and milk. Cover and leave to stand for 30 minutes. • Meanwhile, melt the chocolate over a pan of simmering water and stir in 5 tbsps of the cream. • Whip the rest of the cream until stiff. • Whisk the egg white with the vanilla sugar until stiff and fold into the hazelnuts; add the rum. • Fold half the whipped cream into the nut mixture. • Turn the oven to its lowest setting. • Use the butter and batter to make eight thin pancakes, cooking over a medium heat and turning every two to three minutes, until golden-brown. • Keep the finished pancakes warm in the oven until all the batter is used up. • Brush the pancakes with the melted chocolate, spread the nuts and cream on top and roll them up. • Decorate the pancakes with the rest of the whipped cream and serve on warm plates.

Rhubarb Flans
with
Mango Sauce

Ingredients for four small soufflé dishes:

250g/8oz young rhubarb
Grated rind of ½ a lemon
75g/3oz sugar
½ tsp ground ginger
8 sponge fingers
75g/3oz ground hazelnuts
3 eggs
1 ripe mango
Juice of ½ lemon
125ml/4 fl oz mango syrup

Preparation time:
1½ hours
Cooking time:
35 minutes
Nutritional value:
Analysis per serving, approx:
- 2300kJ/550kcal
- 15g protein
- 32g fat
- 51g carbohydrate

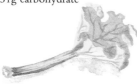

Wash and dry the rhubarb, trim it and remove the strings. • Cut it into 2-cm/¾-inch chunks, sprinkle with the lemon rind, half the sugar and the ginger. Cover and leave at room temperature for one hour. • Crush the sponge fingers between cling film using a rolling pin and mix with the nuts. • Heat the oven to 180°C/350°F/Gas Mark 4. Butter two flan tins and add about a quarter of the nut-and-sponge mixture. • Separate the eggs. Whisk the egg whites until stiff, slowly adding the rest of the sugar and ginger and continue to whisk for another two minutes. • Drain the rhubarb and fold into the egg yolks with the rest of the nut-and-sponge mixture. Lastly, fold in the egg whites and transfer to the flan tins. Place the flan tins in a baking tin half-filled with boiling water. Bake the flans on the middle shelf of the oven for about 35 minutes. • Peel the mango. Cut the flesh away from the

stone, slice and purée it in a mixer with the lemon juice and the mango syrup. Serve the sauce separately with the flans.

Berry Gratin

400g/14oz mixed berries
¹/₄ vanilla pod
4 egg yolks
75g/3oz sugar
Grated rind of ¹/₂ a lemon
125ml/4 fl oz sherry
50g/2oz blanched ground almonds
4 scoops of strawberry sorbet

Preparation time:
30 minutes
Browning time:
4 to 8 minutes
Nutritional value:
Analysis per serving, approx:
• 2900kJ/690kcal
• 21g protein
• 44g fat
• 38g carbohydrate

Wash the berries and leave to drain. • Place three-quarters of the berries in individual ovenproof dishes. Cover the rest and reserve. • Heat the oven to 220°C/425°F/Gas Mark 7. • Split the vanilla pod and scrape out the vanilla. Beat the egg yolks with the vanilla, sugar, lemon rind and sherry over a pan of simmering water until creamy. The mixture should become hot. Fold in the almonds. • Pour the mixture over the berries and bake until golden on the middle shelf of the oven for 4 to 8 minutes. • Decorate the dessert with the remaining berries and serve with a scoop of the sorbet.

Vanilla Soufflé

500g/1lb 2oz raspberries
1 tbsp raspberry liqueur
100g/4oz sugar
5 eggs
1 vanilla pod
Pinch of salt
50g/2oz flour
30g/1oz cornflour
1 tbsp sour cream
2 tbsps lemon juice
1 tsp grated lemon rind
Butter and sugar for the dish
1 tbsp icing sugar to dust

Preparation time:
40 minutes
Baking:
35 minutes
Nutritional value:
Analysis per serving, approx:
• 1900kJ/450kcal
• 19g protein
• 17g fat
• 55g carbohydrate

Wash the raspberries and leave to drain; mix with the raspberry liqueur and 2 tbsps sugar. • Heat the oven to 180°C/350°F/Gas Mark 4.

Butter a soufflé dish and sprinkle with sugar. • Separate the eggs. • Split the vanilla pod, scrape out the vanilla and mix into the egg yolks with half the remaining sugar; beat until fluffy. • Whisk the egg whites with the salt and gradually add the remaining sugar, continuing to beat until stiff. • Mix the flour and all but 1 tsp of the cornflour and stir, with the sour cream, into the egg yolk mixture. Fold in the egg whites. • Put half the beaten mixture into the dish, spread 250g/8oz drained raspberries on top and cover with the remaining mixture. • Bake the soufflé in the middle of the oven for 35 minutes until golden brown. • Cook the remaining raspberries with the juice, the lemon juice and rind as well as 125ml/4 fl oz water, for five minutes, then add the 1 tsp cornflour mixed with a little cold water and bring to the boil again. • Sift icing sugar over the soufflé and serve immediately with the raspberry sauce.

Blood Orange Soufflé

3 blood oranges
3 navel oranges
2 lemons
8 sugar cubes
6 tbsps Grand Marnier
6 sponge fingers
6 eggs
100g/4oz sugar
Butter and sugar for the tin

Preparation time:
1 hour
Baking:
25 minutes
Nutritional value:
Analysis per serving, approx:
- 2500kJ/600kcal
- 23g protein
- 21g fat
- 70g carbohydrate

Peel the blood oranges like an apple, using a sharp knife, and discard the white pith. Divide them into segments, removing the skins, and set aside. Squeeze the navel oranges and reserve the juice. • Wash the lemons in warm water, dry them and rub the peel with the sugar cubes. • Squeeze the lemons and boil the juice with that of the oranges and the sugar cubes until a thickened syrup forms. • Sprinkle the orange segments with half the liqueur, cover and set aside. • Brush a soufflé dish with butter and sprinkle with sugar. • Arrange the sponge fingers in the dish and sprinkle the rest of the liqueur over them. • Heat the oven to 250°C/500°F/Gas Mark 9. • Separate the eggs. Stir the sugar into the egg yolks and then beat over a pan of hot water until fluffy. • Mix the fruit syrup with the yolk mixture and stir over a pan of cold water until cool. • Whisk the egg whites until stiff, fold into the egg yolk mixture and pour into the dish. • Bake for about 10 minutes on the middle shelf of the oven, then reduce the temperature to

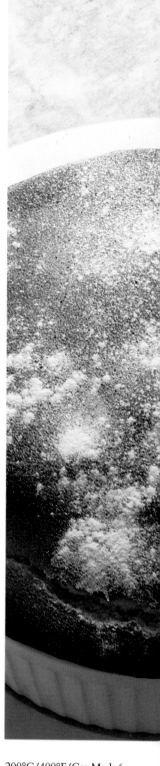

200°C/400°F/Gas Mark 6. Bake the soufflé for a further 15 minutes. • Serve immediately or it will collapse quickly. Serve the orange segments as an accompaniment.

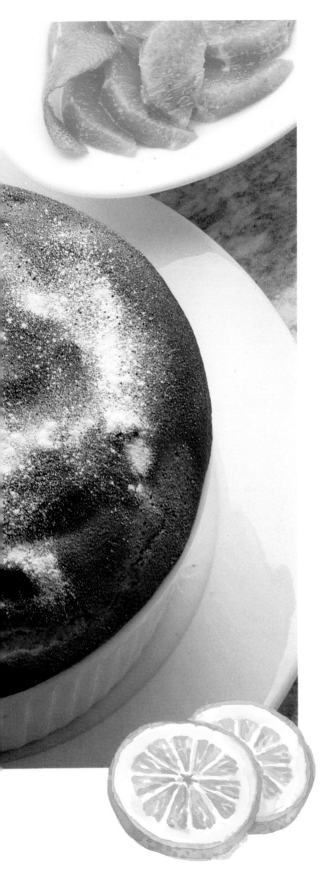

Baked Apples Flambé

4 large cooking apples
100g/4oz sultanas
2 tbsps rum
50g/2oz chopped hazelnuts
125g/5oz marzipan
Generous pinch of ground
cinnamon
1 tbsp vanilla sugar
1/2 lemon
4 tbsps Calvados or cognac

Preparation time:
20 minutes
Baking:
30 minutes
Nutritional value:
Analysis per serving, approx:
• 1700kJ/400kcal
• 5g protein
• 15g fat
• 56g carbohydrate

Heat the oven to 200°C/400°F/Gas Mark 6. Line a baking tin with baking parchment. • Wash, dry and core the apples, using a corer. • Rinse the sultanas in hot water, pat dry and mix with the rum and chopped hazelnuts. • Dice the marzipan, mix with cinnamon and vanilla sugar and then add to the sultanas. • Rinse the lemon in warm water, dry it, grate the rind and squeeze out the juice. • Mix the juice and rind with the marzipan mixture. • Fill the apples with this mixture, place on the baking sheet and bake on the middle shelf of the oven for 30 minutes. • Arrange the baked apples in dessert bowls. When serving, warm the Calvados in a ladle over a candle at the table, ignite and sprinkle over the baked apples.

Our Tip: *Instead of setting light to the apples, they may be served with a zabaglione sauce.*

Apricot Dessert with Cracked Wheat

500g/1lb 2oz *fresh apricots*
80g/3½ oz *cracked wheat*
100g/4oz *coarsely chopped*
almonds
100g/4oz *honey*
250ml/8 fl oz *single cream*
½ tsp *vanilla essence*

Preparation time:
30 minutes
Nutritional value:
Analysis per serving, approx:
• 2400kJ/570kcal
• 10g protein
• 34g fat
• 55g carbohydrate

Wash the apricots in lukewarm water, dry well, halve and stone them. Cut the apricot halves into quarters. • Roast the cracked wheat and almonds in a heavy based, dry frying pan over a medium heat, turning constantly, until they darken and have a pleasant smell. • Add the prepared apricots and the honey and continue heating while stirring until the honey begins to caramelise. • Mix the cream and vanilla into the wheat and simmer, stirring, for another minute. • Transfer the dessert to a heated serving dish and serve while warm.

Our Tip: *As an alternative to apricots, the dessert can be prepared with peaches, nectarines or plums.*

Cherry Fritters
with Vanilla Sauce

For the fritters:
1 egg
150g/5½oz flour
½ packet dried yeast
125ml/4 fl oz beer (not chilled)
Pinch of salt
1 tsp ground cinnamon
1 heaped tbsp sugar
250g/8oz sweet cherries with stalks
For the sauce:
½ vanilla pod
200ml/6 fl oz cream
3 eggs
1 heaped tbsp sugar
Pinch of salt
3 tbsps rum
Oil for deep frying

Preparation time:
1½ hours
Nutritional value:
Analysis per serving, approx:
• 3300kJ/790kcal
• 19g protein
• 53g fat
• 51g carbohydrate

Separate the egg . • Mix the flour with the yeast, beer, salt, cinnamon, sugar and egg yolk. • Whisk the egg white until stiff, fold into the mixture and leave the batter, covered, for one hour. • Wash and pat dry the cherries, but leave the stalks on. • Tie the cherries together in bundles of three. • Split the vanilla pod and scrape out the vanilla; mix both with the cream and bring briefly to the boil. • Blend the eggs with the sugar and salt until creamy. • Strain the cream, slowly stir it into the egg mixture and heat until the sauce has thickened. • Mix the vanilla sauce with the rum and keep warm. • Heat the oil to 180°C/350°F/Gas Mark 4. • Dip the cherry bunches into the batter and fry in the hot oil until golden. • Serve the sauce with the cherries.

Stuffed Peaches

4 large peaches
125 ml/4 fl oz water
100g/4oz sugar
1/2 a lemon
3 egg whites
Pinch of ground cinnamon
4 tbsps redcurrant jelly or
raspberry jam
50g/2oz chopped almonds

Preparation time:
15 minutes
Baking:
10 minutes
Nutritional value:
Analysis per serving, approx:
• 1300kJ/310kcal
• 12g protein
• 8g fat
• 50g carbohydrate

Heat the oven to 240°C/475°F/Gas Mark 9. Line a baking tin with baking parchment. • Prick the peaches with a fork several times, immerse briefly in boiling water and remove the skins; cut in half and remove the stones. • Mix 50g/2oz sugar with the water. Squeeze the lemon and add the juice to the water. Add the peaches and stew, covered, for 7 minutes on a low heat. • Whisk the egg whites until stiff, pour the remaining sugar and cinnamon into them and beat well for a further 2 minutes. • Mix the jelly or jam and chopped almonds and spoon into the drained peach halves. • Place the peaches on the baking sheet, spoon some whipped egg white over them and form small peaks. • Bake the peaches on the top shelf for 10 minutes. Serve immediately.

Banana Kisses

125g/5oz icing sugar
2 egg whites
1 tsp lemon juice
2 bananas
15g/¹/₂ oz butter
2 tbsps chocolate vermicelli
Baking parchment and oil for
the baking sheet

Preparation time:
40 minutes
Baking time:
2 hours
Nutritional value:
Analysis per serving, approx:
• 1200kJ/290kcal
• 7g protein
• 6g fat
• 51g carbohydrate

Heat the oven to 100°C/200°F/Gas Mark ¼. Lightly oil a baking sheet and line it with baking parchment. • Sift the icing sugar onto a piece of greaseproof paper. • Whisk the egg whites and lemon juice until stiff, gradually add the icing sugar, and continue whisking until the egg whites are shiny. • Place the egg whites in a piping bag with a plain nozzle and pipe four banana-shaped strips onto the baking paper. • Place the meringues on the middle shelf of the oven for two hours, keeping the oven door ajar with the handle of a wooden spoon; this dries out the meringue as opposed to baking it. • Peel the bananas and cut in half lengthways. • Melt the butter in a pan and gently fry the bananas on both sides until they begin to caramelise. • Arrange the bananas on the meringues and sprinkle with chocolate strands.

Austrian Quark Soufflé

Ingredients for 6 individual soufflé dishes:

For the apricot sauce:
500g/1lb 2oz ripe apricots
250ml/8 fl oz dry white wine
½ cinnamon stick
2 cloves

For the soufflés:
4 eggs
100g/4oz sugar
Pinch of salt
200g/7oz quark or low fat curd cheese
1 vanilla pod
2 tbsps rum
Grated rind of ½ a lemon
1 tbsp icing sugar to dust
Butter for the soufflé dishes

Preparation time:
40 minutes
Baking:
20 – 30 minutes
Nutritional value:
Analysis per serving, approx:
• 1400kJ/330kcal
• 14g protein
• 12g fat
• 32g carbohydrate

Wash, dry, halve and stone the apricots. Stew gently in the wine, cinnamon and cloves for 10 minutes and then purée in a mixer. • Cover the apricot sauce and reserve it. • Separate the eggs. Beat the egg yolks and sugar until fluffy. Whisk the egg whites with the salt until stiff. • Add the quark to the egg yolks. • Split the vanilla pod and scrape out the vanilla; mix with the rum, lemon rind and quark, and stir into the egg yolks. • Heat the oven to 180°C/350°F/Gas Mark 4. Butter the dishes. • Fold the egg whites into the quark mixture. Divide this between the dishes and stand them in a baking dish filled with hot water. Bake on the middle shelf of the oven for 20 to 30 minutes or until the soufflés are golden. • Dust with icing sugar and serve immediately with the apricot sauce.

Omelette Surprise

Ingredients for 10 portions:
7 eggs
100g/4oz caster sugar
Grated rind of 1 lemon
1 tbsp cognac
100g/4oz flour
25g/1oz each of chopped
almonds and chopped pistachios
20 scoops of ice cream and
sorbet (mixed flavours)
100g/4oz icing sugar, sifted

Preparation time:
40 minutes
Baking time:
12 to 15 minutes
Freezing time:
30 minutes
Nutritional value:
Analysis per serving, approx:
• 1840kJ/440kcal
• 14g protein
• 21g fat
• 46g carbohydrate

Heat the oven to 200°C/400°F/Gas Mark 6. Line a rectangular tin with baking parchment. • Separate the eggs and reserve three of the whites. • Beat the egg yolks with the sugar and lemon rind until fluffy and add the cognac. • Sift the flour into the egg yolk mixture and mix gently. Whisk the four egg whites until stiff and fold into the egg yolks. Spread the mixture evenly over the lined baking tin. • Scatter the almonds and pistachios over the sponge and bake for 12 to 15 minutes until golden; then leave to cool. • Line the bottom of an oblong ovenproof dish with sponge cut to fit. • Arrange the scoops of ice cream over it and cover with the rest of the sponge. • Place the mould in the freezer for 30 minutes so that ice cream does not melt. • Heat the oven to 225°C/425°F/Gas Mark 7. • Whisk the remaining egg whites until stiff, sift 50g/2oz icing sugar over them and fold in. Fold in the other half of the sifted icing sugar and put this meringue into a piping bag with a star nozzle. • Completely cover the sponge

in the mould with egg whites. Place the egg whites on the uppermost shelf of the oven and bake for 4 to 7 minutes until golden. • Serve the omelette at once.

51

Red Wine Pears
with Vanilla Ice Cream

1 lemon
500ml/16 fl oz dry red wine
100g/4oz sugar
1 cinnamon stick
4 small firm pears
500g/1lb 2oz vanilla ice
cream

Preparation time:
20 minutes
Cooking time:
50 minutes
Nutritional value:
Analysis per serving, approx:
• 1890kJ/450kcal
• 8g protein
• 13g fat
• 60g carbohydrate

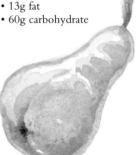

Wash and dry the lemon, slice it and put in an uncovered saucepan with the red wine, sugar and cinnamon stick. Boil until the liquid has reduced slightly. • Wash, dry and peel the pears, using a sharp knife to cut out the cores from the underside. Leave the stalks on the pears if possible. • Remove the cinnamon stick and lemon from the red wine. Stand the pears vertically in a suitable saucepan, add the red wine and cover with a lid; gently simmer for 30 minutes. • Remove the pears, drain them, reserving the liquid, and leave to cool. Boil the red wine liquid until syrupy, in an uncovered saucepan. Allow to cool. • Cut the ice cream into cubes and place in four dessert bowls. Arrange the pears on the ice cream and pour the red wine syrup over them.

Chocolate Banana Sundae

3 egg yolks
1 tbsp vanilla sugar
100g/4oz sugar
150g/5¹/₂oz plain chocolate
¹/₂ tsp cornflour
1 tsp cocoa powder
350ml/14 fl oz milk
250ml/8 fl oz whipping cream
2 ripe bananas
1 tbsp lemon juice
50g/2oz dried banana chips
25g/1 oz chocolate shavings

Preparation time:
45 minutes
Freezing time:
2 hours
Nutritional value:
Analysis per serving, approx:
• 2600kJ/620kcal
• 19g protein
• 66g fat
• 85g carbohydrate

Beat the egg yolks with the vanilla sugar and 75g/3oz sugar until fluffy. • Coarsely grate the chocolate, fold into the egg yolks with the cornflour and cocoa powder and slowly add the milk. Heat the mixture gently, whisking constantly, and bring to the boil. Remove from the heat at once. • Place the saucepan in a bowl of ice water containing ice cubes, and stir until the mixture has cooled. • Beat 125ml/4 fl oz cream with the remaining sugar until stiff and fold into the cooled chocolate mixture. Cover with foil and leave in the freezer for two hours until set. • During the first 30 minutes stir the ice cream twice. • Peel the bananas, mash with a fork and mix with the lemon juice. • Whip the remaining cream until stiff and mix with the bananas. • Place the ice cream in sundae glasses and decorate with the banana cream, banana chips and chocolate shavings.

Raspberry Bomb Glacée

Ingredients for a 1.4l/2½-pint mould:
400g/14oz raspberries
5 tbsps raspberry liqueur
2 tbsps sugar
500ml/16 fl oz whipping cream
4 eggs
100g/4oz sugar
2 tbsps vanilla sugar
50g/2oz plain chocolate
1 tsp cocoa powder
125ml/4 fl oz cream, whipped
50g/2oz crystallised fruits

Preparation time:
1 hour
Freezing time:
14 hours
Nutritional value:
Analysis per serving (serves 8):
• 1970kJ/470kcal
• 9g protein
• 37g fat
• 35g carbohydrate

Wash and drain the raspberries; add half to the liqueur, cover and reserve. • Mix the other raspberries with the sugar. • Whip the 16 fl oz cream until stiff. Mix the eggs and sugar over a pan of simmering water, beating until thick. Remove from the heat and fold in the 16 fl oz whipped cream. • Mix a third of the resulting cream with the vanilla sugar, place in a metal bowl and leave to set in the freezer. • Finely grate the chocolate and stir into the second third of the mixture with the cocoa powder. • Strain the sugared raspberries through a sieve. Mix the raspberry purée into the rest of the cream mixture. Place both mixtures in separate metal bowls and leave to set in the freezer. • Spoon the semi-frozen vanilla mixture into a well-chilled bombe mould and place in the freezer for 30 minutes. • Spread the chocolate cream over the vanilla cream and freeze for 30 minutes, then add the raspberry cream. • Scrape out a hollow in the middle of the final layer and fill it with the

marinated raspberries; cover
with the ice cream scrapings. •
Freeze the bombe glacée for
about 12 hours. Turn out the
bombe glacée and decorate
with the cream and fruit.

55

Ice Cream Gateau
on a Meringue Base

Ingredients for a 24cm/10-inch
springform cake tin:
For the meringue base:
125ml/4 fl oz egg white
(about 4 eggs)
150g/5¹/₂oz caster sugar
100g/4oz icing sugar
2 tbsps cornflour
For the gateau:
100g/4oz sultanas
125ml/4 fl oz rum
1 tbsp lemon juice
6 egg yolks
100g/4oz icing sugar
2 tbsps vanilla sugar
¹/₂ vanilla pod
1 l/1 ³/₄ pints whipping cream
150g/5¹/₂oz plain chocolate
100g/4oz coating chocolate
50g/2oz chocolate shavings

Preparation time:
1½ hours

Baking time:
3 hours
Freezing time:
5 hours
Nutritional value:
Analysis per serving (serves 12):
• 2730kJ/650kcal
• 14g protein
• 38g fat
• 44g carbohydrate

Whisk the egg whites until
stiff and continue
whisking while slowly adding
the caster sugar until glossy.
Sift the icing sugar and
cornflour over the egg whites
and fold in with a metal spoon.
• Heat the oven to
100°C/212°F/Gas Mark ¼.
Line a baking sheet with
baking parchment. • Place the
cake tin on the baking sheet
and trace its shape with a
pencil. • Put the meringue into

56

a piping bag with a star nozzle and fill in the marked circle with a spiral of meringue. • Place on the middle shelf of the oven and dry, rather than bake, for three hours. Keep the oven door ajar with the handle of a wooden spoon. • Wash the sultanas in hot water and drain them. Pour rum and lemon juice over the sultanas. • Beat the egg yolks with the icing sugar and vanilla sugar until white and fluffy. • Split the vanilla pod lengthways, scrape out the inside and mix into the egg yolk mixture. • Beat 600ml/18 fl oz cream until stiff and fold half of it into the vanilla mixture. Place this in the spring form tin and place in the freezer. • Break the chocolate and the coating chocolate into pieces and melt together over a pan of simmering water, stirring in 200ml/6 fl oz un-whipped cream. Cool and add the rum from the sultanas and the rest of the whipped cream. • Arrange the sultanas on the vanilla ice cream and spread the chocolate cream on top. • Whip the rest of the cream until stiff and place in a piping bag with a star nozzle. • Loosen the edge of the gateau with a knife, hold the base of the mould briefly over steam, remove sides of the tin and slide the ice cream gateau onto the cold meringue base. Mark 12 portions on the gateau. Decorate each with a garland of cream and the chocolate shavings. • Keep the gateau in the freezer until it is to be served.

Chocolate Ice Cream

Ingredients for 8 portions:
225g/1oz plain chocolate
2 eggs
2 egg yolks
100g/4oz sugar
750ml/24 fl oz milk
2 tsps instant coffee powder
2 tbsps orange liqueur

Preparation time:
40 minutes
Freezing time:
20 minutes
Nutritional value:
Analysis per serving, approx:
• 1590kJ/380kcal
• 12g protein
• 23g fat
• 32g carbohydrate

Break the chocolate into small pieces. • Use an electric beater and a metal bowl to beat the eggs, egg yolks and half the sugar until creamy. • Bring the milk and the rest of the sugar to the boil, stirring. Dissolve the chocolate and coffee powder in the milk. • Slowly add the boiling milk to the egg-and-sugar mixture, using a whisk. Prepare a bowl of ice water, containing ice cubes. Stand the bowl of ice cream mixture in the bowl of ice water and stir frequently until cold. • Place the cold mixture in the ice cream maker and follow the maker's instructions for freezing until thick and creamy. Towards the end of the freezing time, pour the orange liqueur into the rotating drum and mix into the ice cream for two to three minutes.

Our Tip: *Decorate the ice cream with chopped hazelnuts, grated chocolate or chocolate caraque, as desired.*

Nut Ice Cream

Ingredients for 8 portions:
100g/4oz shelled hazelnuts
½ vanilla pod
1 egg
4 egg yolks
150g/5½oz sugar
500ml/16 fl oz milk
250ml/8 fl oz cream
100g/4oz nut paste

Preparation time:
1¼ hours
Freezing time:
20 minutes
Nutritional value:
Analysis per serving, approx:
• 2300kJ/550kcal
• 15g protein
• 40g fat
• 33g carbohydrate

Roast the hazelnuts in a dry pan turning constantly until the brown skins burst. • Rub the nuts in a tea-towel until all the skins have come off. Grind or chop finely. • Split the vanilla pod lengthways and scrape out the inside. • Beat the egg, egg yolks, half the sugar and the vanilla in a metal bowl over a pan of simmering water until creamy, using an electric beater. • Bring the milk, cream and the rest of the sugar to the boil, stirring constantly, and dissolve the nut paste. • Slowly add the boiling liquid to the egg and sugar mixture over the simmering water, still beating with the electric beater. Add the chopped or ground hazelnuts. Prepare a bowl of ice water, containing ice cubes. Stand the bowl of ice cream mixture in the bowl of ice water and stir frequently until cold. • Place the mixture in the ice cream maker and follow the instructions for freezing until the ice cream is thick and creamy. This will take about 20 minutes.

Citrons Givrés

Ingredients for 8 portions:
8 large, lemons
250ml/8 fl oz dry white wine
150g/5¹/₂oz sugar
1 egg white
Pinch of salt
50g/2oz candied lemon peel
2 tbsp orange liqueur

Preparation time:
30 minutes
Freezing time:
4¹/₂ hours
Nutritional value:
Analysis per serving, approx:
• 710kJ/170kcal
• 2g protein
• 5g fat
• 32g carbohydrate

Wash the lemons in warm water, dry them and cut a slice from the long side of each. Remove the flesh and wrap the empty skins and severed slices in aluminium foil and freeze. • Gently simmer the wine and sugar for five minutes, stirring, and allow to cool. • Remove the pith, pips and inner membranes from the lemon, but leave the fine skin between the segments as this provides extra taste. • Purée the flesh in a liquidiser or food processor. Mix with the cold wine, place in a metal bowl, cover with aluminium foil and leave to set in the freezer for four hours. • After nearly four hours whip the egg white with the salt until stiff. Dice the candied lemon peel finely and fold into the egg white with the liqueur. • Place the frozen fruit mixture in the liquidiser or food processor, grind finely then fold in the flavoured egg white. • Spoon the mixture into the lemon skins, top with a lid and place the lemons in the freezer for a further 30 minutes. • Remove the lemons from the freezer 15 minutes before serving.

Our Tip: *The same dessert can be prepared using oranges or mandarins.*

Redcurrant and Kiwi Sorbet

Ingredients for 8 portions:
250g/8oz caster sugar
100ml/3 fl oz water
300g/10oz redcurrants
4 kiwis
2 tbsps cassis (blackcurrant liqueur)
125ml/4 fl oz dry red wine
125ml/4 fl oz dry sparkling white wine
1 tbsp white rum
2 egg whites

Preparation time:
40 minutes
Freezing time:
2 hours
Nutritional value:
Analysis per serving, approx:
• 880kJ/210kcal
• 4g protein
• 0g fat
• 41g carbohydrate

Heat the sugar and water, boil for five minutes and then allow to cool. • Wash and drain the redcurrants and reserve some sprigs for decoration. Remove stalks from the rest of the redcurrants and purée also. • Peel three kiwis, cut into pieces and purée. Mix half the sugar syrup into each purée. • Add the cassis and red wine to the redcurrant purée and mix the white wine and rum into the kiwi purée. • Place both purées in separate metal bowls, cover and freeze for one hour until almost set, stirring at 15-minute intervals. • Whisk the egg whites until stiff and fold half into each of the purées. Freeze the sorbets for another hour. • Peel the fourth kiwi fruit and cut into slices. • Arrange one scoop of each sorbet in individual dessert bowls or wine glasses and decorate with slices of kiwi and the reserved redcurrants.

Passion Fruit and Persimmon Sorbet

250ml/8 fl oz water
Juice of 1 lemon
125g/5oz caster sugar
2 fully ripe persimmons (kaki or sharon fruit)
2 passion fruits
2 tbsps apricot liqueur
1 egg white
1 tbsp vanilla sugar

Preparation time:
45 minutes
Freezing time:
2 hours
Nutritional value:
Analysis per serving, approx:
• 1000kJ/240kcal
• 5g protein
• 0g fat
• 52g carbohydrate

Boil the water, lemon juice and sugar for five minutes, then allow to cool. • Peel the persimmons and strain through a sieve. Halve the passion fruit, scoop out the contents with a teaspoon and mix with the persimmon purée. • Mix the purée with the sugar syrup and liqueur, place in a metal bowl, cover and freeze for about an hour until nearly set, stirring at short intervals. • Whisk the egg white until fluffy, gradually pour in the vanilla sugar and continue whisking until stiff and shiny. • Fold the egg whites into the fruit purée and freeze the sorbet for another hour. • Arrange scoops of sorbet in individual dessert dishes or wine glasses.

Index